WAITING FOR A VISA

Dr. B.R. Ambedkar

THE MILKY WAY
PUBLICATIONS

ISBN: 978-81-987275-3-4

Publisher: The Milky Way Publications
Mumbai, Maharashtra

Phone: +91 9167080475
WhatsApp: +91 9167080475
E-mail: themilkywaypublications@gmail.com

First Edition: 2025

WAITING FOR A VISA
Dr. B.R. Ambedkar

Table of Content

PREFACE

Foreigners of course know of the existence of untouchability. But not being next door to it, so to say, they are unable to realise how oppressive it is in its actuality. It is difficult for them to understand how it is possible for a few untouchables to live on the edge of a village consisting of a large number of Hindus; go through the village daily to free it from the most disagreeable of its filth and to carry the errands of all and sundry; collect food at the doors of the Hindus; buy spices and oil at the shops of the Hindu Bania from a distance; regard the village in every way as their home— and yet never touch or be touched by any one belonging to the village. The problem is how best to give an idea of the way the untouchables are treated by the caste Hindus. A general description or a record of cases and of the treatment accorded to them are the two methods by which this purpose could be achieved. I have felt that the latter would be more effective than the former. In choosing these illustrations I have drawn partly upon my experience and partly upon the experience of others. I begin with events that have happened to me in my own life.

- Dr. B.R. Ambedkar

A Childhood Journey to Koregaon Becomes A Nightmare

Our family came originally from Dapoli Taluka of the Ratnagiri District of the BombayPresidency. From the very commencement of the rule of the East India Company, my forefathers had left their hereditary occupation for service in the Army of the Company. My father also followed the family tradition and sought service in the Army. He rose to the rank of an officer, and was a Subhedar when he retired. On his retirement my father took the family to Dapoli with a view to settling down there. But for some reason my father changed his mind. The family left Dapoli for Satara, where we lived till 1904.

The first incident, which I am recording as well as I can remember, occurred in about 1901, when we were at Satara. My mother was then dead. My father was away on service as a cashier at a place called Koregaon in Khatav Taluka in the Satara District, where the Government of Bombay had started the work of excavating a Tank [=artificial reservoir] so as to give employment to famine-stricken people, who were dying by thousands.

When my father went to Koregaon he left me, my brother who was older than myself, and two sons of my eldest sister (who was dead), in charge of my aunt and some kind neighbours. My aunt was the kindest soul I know, but she was of no help to us. She was somewhat of a dwarf and had some trouble with her legs, which made it very difficult for her to move about without somebody's aid. Oftentimes she had to be lifted. 1 had sisters. They were married and were away living with their families.

Cooking our food became a problem with us, especially since our aunty could not, on account of her helplessness, manage the job. We four children went to school, and we also cooked our food. We could not prepare bread. So we lived on Pulav—which we found to be the easiest dish to prepare, requiring nothing more than mixing rice and mutton.

Being a cashier, my father could not leave his station to come to Satara to see us; therefore he wrote to us to come to Koregaon and spend our summer vacation with him. We children were thoroughly excited over the prospect, especially as none of us had up to that time seen a railway train.

Great preparations were made. New shirts of English make [=style], bright bejewelled caps, new shoes, new silk-bordered dhoties [=wrapped lower garments], were ordered for the journey.

My father had given us all the particulars regarding our journey, and had told us to inform him on which day we were starting, so that he would send his peon [=errand-runner] to the Railway Station to meet us and to take us to Koregaon. According to this arrangement myself, my brother, and one of my sister's sons left Satara, our aunt remaining in the charge of our neighbours, who promised to look after her.

The Railway Station was ten miles distant from our place, and a tonga (a one-horse carriage) was engaged to take us to the Station. We were dressed in the new clothing specially made for the occasion, and we left our home full of joy—but amidst the cries of my aunt, who was almost prostrate with grief at our parting.

When we reached the station my brother bought tickets, and gave me and my sister's son two annas each as pocket money, to be spent at our pleasure. We at once began our career of riotous living, and .each ordered a bottle of lemonade at the start. After a short while the train whistled in and we boarded it as quickly as we could, for fear of being left behind. We were told to detrain at Masur, the nearest railway station for Koregaon.

The train arrived at Masur at about five in the evening, and we got down with our luggage. In a few minutes all the passengers who had got down from the train had gone away to their destinations. We four children remained on the platform, looking out for my father or his servant whom he had promised to send. Long did we wait—but no one turned up. An hour elapsed, and the station-master came to enquire. He asked us for our tickets. We showed them to him. He asked us why we tarried.

We told him that we were bound for Koregaon, and that we were waiting for father or his servant to come, but that neither had turned up, and that we did not know how to reach Koregaon. We were well-dressed children. From our dress or talk no one could make out that we were children of the untouchables. Indeed the station- master was quite sure we were Brahmin children, and was extremely touched at the plight in which he found us.

As is usual among the Hindus, the station-master asked us who we were. Without a moment's thought I blurted out that we were Mahars. (Mahar is one of the communities which are treated as untouchables in the Bombay Presidency). He was stunned. His face underwent a sudden change. We could see that he was overpowered by a strange feeling of repulsion. As soon as he heard my reply he went away to his room, and we stood where we were. Fifteen to twenty minutes elapsed; the sun was almost setting. Our father had not turned up, nor had he sent his servant; and now the station- master had also left us. We were quite bewildered, and the joy and happiness which we had felt at the beginning of the journey gave way to a feeling of extreme sadness.

After half an hour, the station-master returned and asked us what we proposed to do. We said that if we could get a bullock-cart on hire, we would go to Koregaon; and if it was not very far, we would like to start straightway. There were many bullock-carts plying for hire. But my reply to the station-master that we were Mahars had gone round among the cartmen, and not one of them was prepared to suffer being polluted, and to demean himself carrying passengers of the untouchable classes. We were prepared to pay double the fare, but we found that money did not work.

The station-master who was negotiating on our behalf stood silent, not knowing what to do. Suddenly a thought seemed to have entered his head and he asked us, "Can you drive the cart?" Feeling that he was finding out a solution of our difficulty, we shouted, "Yes, we can." With that answer he went and proposed on our behalf that we were to pay the cartman double the fare and drive the cart, and that he should walk on foot along with the cart on our journey. One cartman agreed, since it gave him an opportunity to earn his fare and also saved him from being polluted.

It was about 6:30 p.m. when we were ready to start. But we were anxious not to leave the station until we were assured that we would reach Koregaon before it was dark. We therefore questioned the cartman about the distance, and the time he would take to reach Koregaon. He assured us that it would be not more than three hours. Believing in his word, we put our luggage in the cart, thanked the station-master, and got into the cart. One of us took the reins and the cart started, with the man walking by our side.

Not very far from the station there flowed a river. It was quite dry, except at places where there were small pools of water. The owner of the cart proposed that we should halt there and have our meal, as we might not get water on our way. We agreed. He asked us to give a part of his fare to enable him to go to the village and have his meal. My brother gave him some money and he left, promising to return soon. We were very hungry, and were glad to have had an opportunity to have a bite. My aunty had pressed our neighbours' womenfolk into service and had got some nice preparation [of food] for us to take on our way. We opened the tiffin basket and started eating.

We needed water to wash things down. One of us went to the pool of water in the river basin nearby. But the water really was no water. It was thick with mud and urine and excreta of the cows and buffaloes and other cattle who went to the pool for drinking. In fact that water was not intended for human use. At any rate the stink of the water was so strong we could not drink it. We had therefore to close our meal before we were satisfied, and wait for the arrival of the cartman. He did not come for a long time, and all that we could do was to look for him in all directions.

Ultimately he came, and we started on our journey. For some four or five miles we drove the cart and he walked on foot. Then he suddenly jumped into the cart and took the reins from our hand. We thought this to be rather strange conduct on the part of a man who had refused to let the cart on hire for fear of pollution~to have set aside all his religious scruples and to haveconsented to sit with us in the same cart; but we dared not ask him any questions on the point. We were anxious to reach Koregaon, our destination, as quickly as possible. And for some time we were interested in the movement of the cart only.

But soon there was darkness all around us. There were no street lights to relieve the darkness. There were no men or women or even cattle passing by, to make us feel that we were in their midst. We became fearful of the loneliness which surrounded us. Our anxiety was growing. We mustered all the courage we possessed. We had travelled far from Masur. It was more than three hours. But there was no sign of Koregaon.

There arose a strange thought within us. We suspected that the cartman intended treachery, and that he was taking us to some lonely spot to kill us. We had lot of gold ornaments on us, and that helped to strengthen our suspicion. We started asking him how far Koregaon was, and why we were so late in reaching it. He kept on saying, "It is not very far, we shall soon reach it." It was about 10:00 at night when, finding that there was no trace of Koregaon, we children started crying and abusing the cartman. Our lamentations and wailings continued for a long time.

The cartman made no reply.

Suddenly we saw a light burning at some distance. The cartman said, "Do you see that light? That is a light of the toll-collector. We will rest there for the night." We felt some relief and stopped crying. The light was distant, and we could never seem to reach it. It took us two hours to reach the toll-collector's hut. The interval increased our anxiety, and we kept on asking the cartman all sorts of questions, as to why there was delay in reaching the place, whether we were going on the right road, etc.

Ultimately by midnight the cart reached the toll-collector's hut. It was situated at the foot of a hill, but on the other side of the hill. When we arrived we saw a large number of bullock-carts there, all resting for the night. We were extremely hungry, and wanted very much to eat. But again there was the question of water. So we asked our driver whether it was possible to get water. He warned us that the toll-collector was a Hindu, and that there was no possibility of our getting water if we spoke the truth and said that we were Mahars. He said, "Say you are Mohammedans and try your luck."

On his advice I went to the toll-collector's hut and asked him if he would give us some water. "Who are you?" he inquired. I replied that we were Musalmans. I conversed with him in Urdu (which I knew very well), so as to leave no doubt that I was a real Musalman. But the trick did not work and his reply was very curt. "Who has kept water for you? There is water on the hill, if you want to go and get it; I have none." With this he dismissed me. I returned to the cart, and conveyed to my brother his reply. I don't know what my brother felt. All that he did was to tell us to lie down.

The bullocks had been unyoked, and the cart was placed sloping down on the ground. We spread our beds on the bottom planks inside the cart, and laid down our bodies to rest. Now that we had come to a place of safety we did not mind what happened. But our minds could not help turning to the latest event. There was plenty of food with us. There was hunger burning within us; with all this we were to sleep without food; that was because we could get no water, and we could get no water because we were untouchables. Such was the last thought that entered our mind. I said, we had come to a place of safety. Evidently my elder brother had his misgivings. He said it was not wise for all four of us to go to sleep. Anything might happen. He suggested that at one time two should sleep, and two should keep watch. So we spent the night at the foot of that hill.

Early at five in the morning our cartman came, and suggested that we should start for Koregaon. We flatly refused. We told him that we would not move until eight o'clock. We did not want to take any chance[s]. He said nothing. So we left at eight and reached Koregaon at eleven. My father was surprised to see us, and said that he had received no intimation [=information] of our coming. We protested that we had given intimation. He denied the fact. Subsequently it was discovered that the fault was that of my father's servant. He had received our letter, but had failed to give it to my father.

This incident has a very important place in my life. I was a boy of nine when it happened. But it has left an indelible impression on my mind. Before this incident occurred, I knew that I was an untouchable, and that untouchables were subjected to certain indignities and discriminations. For instance, I knew that in the school I could not sit in the midst of my classmates according to my rank [in class performance], but that I was to sit in a corner by myself. I knew that in the school I was to have a separate piece of gunny cloth for me to squat on in the classroom, and the servant employed to clean the school would not touch the gunny cloth used by me. I was required to carry the gunny cloth home in the evening, and bring it back the next day.

While in the school I knew that children of the touchable classes, when they felt thirsty, could go out to the water tap, open it, and quench their thirst. All that was necessary was the permission of the teacher. But my position was separate. I could not touch the tap; and unless it was opened for it by a touchable person, it was not possible for me to quench my thirst. In my case the permission of the teacher was not enough. The presence of the school peon was necessary, for he was the only person whom the class teacher could use for such a purpose. If the peon was not available, 1 had to go without water. The situation can be summed up in the statement—no peon, no water.

At home I knew that the work of washing clothes was done by my sisters. Not that there were no washermen in Satara. Not that we could not afford to pay the washermen. Washing was done by my sisters because we were untouchable,s and no washerman would wash the clothes of an untouchable. The work of cutting our hair or shaving the boys, including myself, was done by our elder sister, who had become quite an expert barber by practising the art on us. Not that there were no barbers in Satara, and not that we could not afford to pay the barber. The work of shaving and hair-cutting was done by my sister because we were untouchables, and no barber would consent to shave an untouchable.

All this I knew. But this incident gave me a shock such as I had never received before, and it made me think about untouchability—which, before this incident happened, was with me a matter of course, as it is with many touchables as well as the untouchables.

Back from the West and Unable to Find Lodging in Baroda

In 1916 I returned to India. I had been sent to America by His Highness the Maharaja of Baroda for higher education. I studied at Columbia University in New York from 1913 to 1917.

In 1917 I came to London and joined the post-graduate department of the School of Economics of the University of London. In 1918 I was obliged to return to India without completing my studies. Since I had been educated by the Baroda State, I was bound to serve the State. [Note: the dates here appear to be a bit confused.] Accordingly, on my arrival I straightway went to Baroda. The reasons why I left Baroda service are quite irrelevant to my present purpose. I do not therefore wish to enter into them. I am only concerned with my social experiences in Baroda, and I will confine myself to describing them.

My five years of staying in Europe and America had completely wiped out of my mind any consciousness that I was an untouchable, and that an untouchable wherever he went in India was a problem to himself and to others. But when I came out of the station, my mind was considerably disturbed by a question, "Where to go? Who will take me?" I felt deeply agitated.

Hindu hotels, called Vishis, I knew there were. They would not take me. The only way of seeking accommodation therein was by impersonation. But I was not prepared for it, because I could well anticipate the dire consequences which were sure to follow if my identity was discovered as it was sure to be.

I had friends in Baroda who had come to America for study. "Would they welcome me if I went?" I could not assure myself. They may [=might] feel embarrassed at admitting an untouchable into their household. I stood under the roof of the station for some time, thinking where to go, what to do. It then struck me to enquire if there was any place in the camp. All [the other] passengers had by this time gone; I alone was left. Some hackney [=carriage] drivers who had failed to pick up any passengers were watching and waiting for me.

I called one of them, and asked him if he knew if there was a hotel in the camp. He said that there was a Parsi inn, and that they took paying guests. Hearing that it was an inn maintained by the Parsis, my heart was gladdened. The Parsis are followers of the Zoroastrian religion. There was no fear of my being treated by them as an untouchable, because their religion does not recognise untouchability. With a heart glad with hope and a mind free from fear, I put my luggage in a hackney carriage and asked the driver to drive me to [the] Parsi inn in the camp.

The inn was a two-storied building, on the ground floor of which lived an old Parsi with his family. He was a caretaker, and supplied food to tourists who came there to stay. The carriage arrived, and the Parsi caretaker showed me upstairs. I went up while the carriage driver brought up my luggage. I paid him and he went away. I felt happy that after all I had solved my problem of finding a place to stay. I was undressing, as I wanted to be at ease. In the meantime the caretaker came with a book in his hand. Seeing as he could well see from my half-undressed state that I had no Sadra and Kasti, the two things which prove that one is a Parsi, in a sharp tone he asked me who I was.

Not knowing that this inn was maintained by the Parsi community for the use of Parsis only, I told him that I was a Hindu. He was shocked, and told me that I could not stay in the inn. I was thoroughly shocked by his answer and was cold all over. The question returned again, where to go? Composing myself, 1 told him that though a Hindu, I had no objection to staying there if he had no objection. He replied, "How can you? 1 have to maintain a register of all those who stay here in the inn." I saw his difficulty. I said 1 could assume a Parsi name for the purpose of entering it in the register. "Why do you object, if I do not object? You will not lose, you will earn something if I stay here."

I could see that he was inclined favourably. Evidently he had had no tourist for a long time and he did not like to forego the opportunity of making a little money. He agreed, on condition that 1 pay him a rupee and a half per day for board and lodging, and enter myself as a Parsi in his register. He went downstairs, and I heaved a sigh of relief. The problem was solved, and I felt very happy. But alas! I did not then know how short was to be this happiness. But before I describe the tragic end of my stay in this inn, 1 must describe how I passed my time during the short period I lived therein.

The inn on the first [=second] floor had a small bed-room, and adjoining it was one small bath room with a water tap in it. The rest was one big hall. At the time of my stay the big hall was filled up with all sorts of rubbish —planks, benches, broken chairs, etc. In the midst of these surroundings I lived, a single solitary individual. The caretaker came up in the morning with a cup of tea. He came again at about 9:30 a.m. with my breakfast or morning meal. A third time he came up at about 8:30 in the evening with my dinner. The caretaker came up only when he could not avoid it, and on these occasions he never stayed to talk to me. The day was spent somehow.

I was appointed as a probationer in the Accountant General's Office by the Maharaja of Baroda. I used to leave the inn at about ten a.m. for the office, and return late at about eight in the evening, contriving to while away outside the inn as much time in [the] company of friends as I could. The idea of returning to the inn to spend the night therein was most terrifying to me, and I used to return to the inn only because I had no other place under the sky to go for rest. In this big hall on the first [=second] floor of the inn there were no fellow human beings to talk to. I was quite alone. The whole hall was enveloped in complete darkness. There were no electric lights, nor even oil lamps to relieve the darkness. The caretaker used to bring up for my use a small hurricane lamp. Its light could not extend beyond a few inches.

I felt that 1 was in a dungeon, and 1 longed for the company of some human being to talk to. But there was no one. In the absence of the company of human beings I sought the company of books, and read and read. Absorbed in reading, I forgot my lonely condition. But the chirping and flying about of the bats, which had made the hall their home, often distracted my mind and sent cold shivers through me˜reminding me of what I was endeavouring to forget, that 1 was in a strange place under strange conditions.

Many a time I must have been angry. But I subdued my grief and my anger through the feeling that though it was a dungeon, it was a shelter, and that some shelter was better than no shelter. So heart-rending was my condition that when my sister's son came from Bombay, bringing my remaining luggage which I had left behind, and when he saw my state, he began to cry so loudly that I had to send him back immediately. In this state I lived in the Parsi inn, impersonating a Parsi.

I knew that I could not long continue this impersonation, as I would be discovered some day. I was therefore trying to get a State bungalow to stay in. But the Prime Minister did not look upon my request with the same urgency [as 1 did]. My petition went from officer to officer—and before 1 got the final reply, the day of my doom arrived.

It was the eleventh day of my stay in the inn. 1 had taken my morning meal, and had dressed up, and was about to step out of my room to go to [the] office. As I was picking up some books which I had borrowed overnight, for returning them to the library, I heard [the] footsteps of a considerable number of people coming up the staircase. I thought they were tourists who had come to stay, and was therefore looking out to see who these friends were. Instantly I saw a dozen angry-looking, tall, sturdy Parsis, each armed with a stick, coming towards my room. I realised that they were not fellow tourists, and they gave proof of it immediately.

They lined up in front of my room and fired a volley of questions. "Who are you? Why did you come here? How dare you take a Parsi name? You scoundrel! You have polluted the Parsi inn!" I stood silent. I could give no answer. I could not persist in impersonation. It was in fact a fraud, and the fraud was discovered, and I am sure if I had persisted in the game I was playing, I would have been assaulted by the mob of angry and fanatic Parsis and probably doomed to death. My meekness and my silence averted this doom. One of them asked when I thought of vacating.

At that time my shelter I prized more than my life. The threat implied in this question was a grave one. I therefore broke my silence and implored them to let me stay for a week at least, thinking that my application to the Minister for a bungalow would be decided upon favourably in the meantime. But the Parsis were in no mood to listen. They issued an ultimatum. They must not find me in the inn in the evening. I must pack off. They held out dire consequences, and left. I was bewildered. My heart sank within me. 1 cursed all, and wept bitterly. After all, I was deprived of my precious possession--namely, my shelter. It was no better than a prisoner's cell. But to me it was very precious.

After the Parsis were gone, I sat for some time engaged in thinking, [seeking] to find a way out. I had hopes that I would soon get a State bungalow, and my troubles would be over. My problem was therefore a temporary problem, and I thought that going to friends would be a good solution. I had no friends among the untouchables of Baroda State. But I had friends among other classes. One was a Hindu, the other was an Indian Christian. I first went to my Hindu friend and told him what had befallen me. He was a noble soul and a great personal friend of mine. He was sad and also indignant. He, however, let fall one observation. He said, "If you come to my home, my servants will go." 1 took the hint, and did not press him to accommodate me.

I did not like to go to the Indian Christian friend. Once he had invited me to go and stay with him. But I had declined, preferring to stay in the Parsi inn. My reason was that his habits were not congenial to me. To go now would be to invite a rebuff. So I went to my office, but I could not really give up this chance of finding a shelter. On consulting a friend 1 decided to go to him [=to the Indian Christian friend] and ask him if he would accommodate me. When I put the question, his reply was that his wife was coming to Baroda the next day, and that he would have to consult her.

I learnt subsequently that it was a very diplomatic answer. He and his wife came originally from a family which was Brahmin by caste, and although on conversion to Christianity the husband had become liberal in thought, the wife had remained orthodox in her ways, and would not have consented to harbour an untouchable in her house. The last ray of hope thus flickered away. It was four p.m. when I left the house of my Indian Christian friend. Where to go was the one supreme question before me. I must quit the inn, and had no friend to go to!! The only alternative left was to return to

Bombay.

The train to Bombay left Baroda at nine p.m. There were five hours to be spent. Where to spend them? Should I go to the inn? Should I go to my friend? I could not muster up sufficient courage to go back to the inn. I feared the Parsis might come and attack me. I did not like to go to my friend. Though my condition was pitiable, I did not like to be pitied. I decided to spend the five hours in the public garden which is called Kamathi Baug, on the border of the city and the camp. I sat there partly with a vacant mind, partly with sorrow at the thought of what had happened to me, and thought of my father and mother as children do when they are in a forlorn condition.

At eight p.m. I came out of the garden, took a carriage to the inn, brought down my luggage. The caretaker came out, but neither he nor 1 could utter a word to each other. He felt that he was in some way responsible for bringing him [=me] into trouble. I paid him his bill. He received it in silence, and I took his leave in silence.

I had gone to Baroda with high hope[s], I had given up many offers. It was wartime. Many places in the Indian Educational service were vacant. I knew very influential people in London. But 1 did not seek any of them. I felt that my duty was to offer my services first to the Maharaja of Baroda, who had financed my education. And here 1 was driven to leave Baroda and return to Bombay, after a stay of only eleven days.

This scene of a dozen Parsis armed with sticks lined [up] before me in a menacing mood, and myself standing before them with a terrified look imploring for mercy, is a scene which so long a period as eighteen years has not succeeded in fading [=causing to fade] away. I can even now vividly recall it~and [I] never recall it without tears in my eyes. It was then for the first time that I learnt that a person who is an untouchable to a Hindu is also an untouchable to a Parsi.

Pride, Awkwardness, and A Dangerous Accident in Chalisgaon

The year was 1929. The Bombay Government had appointed a Committee to investigate the grievances of the untouchables. I was appointed a member of the Committee. The Committee had to tour all over the province to investigate the allegations of injustice, oppression and tyranny. The Committee split up. I and another member were assigned the two districts of Khandesh. My colleague and myself, after finishing our work, parted company. He went to see some Hindu saint. I left by train to go to Bombay. At Chalisgaon I got down to go to a village on the Dhulia line, to investigate a case of social boycott which had been declared by the caste Hindus against the untouchables of that village.

The untouchables of Chalisgaon came to the station and requested me to stay for the night with them. My original plan was to go straight to Bombay after investigating the case of social boycott. But as they were keen [=eager], I agreed to stay overnight. I boarded the train for Dhulia to go to the village, went there and informed myself of the situation prevailing in the village, and returned by the next train to Chalisgaon.

I found the untouchables of Chalisgaon waiting for me at the station. I was garlanded. The Maharwada, the quarters of the untouchables, is about two miles from the Railway Station, and to reach it one has to cross a river on which there is a culvert. There were many horse carriages at the station plying [=available] for hire. The Maharwada was also within walking distance from the station. I expected immediately to be taken to the Maharwada. But there was no movement in that direction, and I could not understand why I was kept waiting.

After an hour or so a tonga (one-horse carriage) was brought close to the platform, and I got in. The driver and I were the only two occupants of the tonga. Others went on foot by a short cut. The tonga had not gone 200 paces when there was almost a collision with a motor car. I was surprised that the driver, who was hired for driving every day, should have been so inexperienced. The accident was averted only because on the loud shout of the policeman the driver of the car pulled it back.

We somehow came to the culvert on the river. On it there are no walls as there are on a bridge. There is only a row of stones fixed at a distance of five or ten feet. It is paved with stones. The culvert on the river is at right angles to the road we were coming by. A sharp turn has to be taken to come to the culvert from the road. Near the very first side stone of the culvert, the horse, instead of going straight, took a turn and bolted. The wheel of the tonga struck against the side stone so forcibly that I was bodily lifted up and thrown down on the stone pavement of the culvert, and the horse and the carriage fell down from the culvert into the river.

So heavy was the fall that I lay down [=there] senseless. The Maharwada is just on the other bank of the river. The men who had come to greet me at the station had reached there ahead of me. I was lifted and taken to the Maharwada amidst the cries and lamentations of the men, women and children. As a result of this I received several injuries. My leg was fractured, and I was disabled for several days. I could not understand how all this had happened. The tongas pass and repass the culvert every day, and never has a driver failed to take the tonga safely over the culvert.

On enquiry I was told the real facts. The delay at the railway station was due to the fact that the tongawalas were not prepared to drive the tonga with a passenger who was an untouchable. It was beneath their dignity. The Mahars could not tolerate that I should walk to their quarters. It was not in keeping with their sense of my dignity. A compromise was therefore arrived at. That compromise was to this effect: the owner of the tonga would give the tonga on hire, but not drive. The Mahars may [=could] take the tonga, but must find someone to drive it.

The Mahars thought this to be a happy solution. But they evidently forgot that the safety of the passenger was more important than the maintenance of his dignity. If they had thought of this, they would have considered whether they could get a driver who could safely conduct me to my destination. As a matter of fact none of them could drive, because it was not their trade. They therefore asked someone from amongst themselves to drive. The man took the reins in his hand and started, thinking there was nothing in it. But as he got on [=went along], he felt his responsibility and became so nervous that he gave up all attempt to [=at]control. To save my dignity, the Mahars of Chalisgaon had put my very life in jeopardy. It is [=was] then I learnt that a Hindu tongawalla, no better than a menial, has a dignity by which he can look upon himself as a person who is superior to any untouchable, even though he may be a Barristerat-law.

Polluting the Water in the Fort of Daulatabad

In the year 1934, some of my co-workers in the movement of the depressed classes expressed a desire to go on a sight-seeing tour, if I agreed to join them. I agreed. It was decided that our plan should at all events include a visit to the Buddhist caves at Verul. It was arranged that I should go to Nasik, and the party should join me at Nasik. To go to Verul we had to go to Aurangabad. Aurangabad is a town in the Mohammedan State of Hyderabad, and is included in the dominion of His Exalted Highness, the Nizam.

On the way to Aurangabad we had first to pass another town called Daulatabad, which is also in the Hyderabad State. Daulatabad is a historical place and was, at one time, the capital of a famous Hindu King, by name Ramdeo Rai. The fort of Daulatabad is an ancient historical monument,, and no tourist while in that vicinity should omit a visit to it. Accordingly our party had also included in its programme a visit to the fort of Daulatabad.

We hired some buses and touring cars. We were about thirty in number. We started from Nasik to Yeola, as Yeola is on the way to Aurangabad. Our tour programme had not been announced—and quite deliberately. We wanted to travel incognito, in order to avoid difficulties which an untouchable tourist has to face in outlying parts of the country. We had informed only our people at those centres at which we had decided to halt. Accordingly, although on the way we passed many villages in the Nizam's State, none of our people had come to meet us.

It was naturally different at Daulatabad. There our people had been informed that we were coming. They were waiting for us and had gathered at the entrance to the town. They asked us to get down and have tea and refreshment first, and then to go to see the fort. We did not agree to their proposal. We wanted tea very badly, but we wanted sufficient time to see the fort before it was dusk. We therefore left for the fort, and told our people that we would take tea on our return.

Accordingly we told our drivers to move on, and within a few minutes we were at the gate of the fort.

The month was Ramjan, the month of fast for the Mohammedans. Just outside the gate of the fort there is a small tank of water full to the brim. There is all around a wide stone pavement. Our faces, bodies and clothes were full of dust gathered in the course of our journey, and we all wished to have a wash. Without much thought, some members of the party washed their faces and their legs on the pavement with the water from the tank. After these ablutions, we went to the gate of the fort. There were armed soldiers inside. They opened the big gates and admitted us into the archway.

We had just commenced asking the guard the

procedure for obtaining permission to go into the fort. In the meantime an old Mohammedan with [a] white flowing beard was coming from behind shouting "The Dheds (meaning untouchables) have polluted the tank!" Soon all the young and old Mohammedans who were nearabout joined him and all started abusing us. "The Dheds have become arrogant. The Dheds have forgotten their religion (i.e. to remain low and degraded).

The Dheds must be taught a lesson." They assumed a most menacing mood.

We told them that we were outsiders and did not know the local custom. They turned the fire of their wrath against the local untouchables, who by that time had arrived at the gate. "Why did you not tell these outsiders that this tank could not be used by untouchables?" was the question they kept on asking them. Poor people! They were not there when we entered [the] tank [area]. It was really our mistake, because we acted without inquiry. The local untouchables protested that it was not their fault.

But the Mohammedans were not prepared to listen to my explanation. They kept on abusing them and us. The abuse was so vulgar that it exasperated us. There could easily have been a riot, and possibly murders. We had, however, to restrain ourselves. We did not want to be involved in a criminal case which would bring our tour to an abrupt end.

One young Muslim in the crowd kept on saying

that everyone must conform to his religion, meaning thereby that the untouchables must not take water from a public tank. I had grown quite impatient, and asked him in a somewhat angry tone, "Is that what your religion teaches? Would you prevent an untouchable from taking water from this tank if he became a Mohammedan?"

These straight questions seemed to have some effect on the Mohammedans. They gave no answer, and stood silent. Turning to the guard I said, again in an angry tone, "Can we get into the fort or not? Tell us; if we can't, we don't want to stop [=stay]." The guard asked for my name. I wrote it out on a piece of paper. He took it to the Superintendent inside, and came out. We were told that we could go into the fort, but we could not touch water anywhere in the fort; and an armed soldier was ordered to go with us to see that we did not transgress the order.

I gave one instance to show that a person who is an untouchable to a Hindu is also an untouchable to a Parsi. This will show that a person who is an untouchable to a Hindu is also an untouchable to a Mohammedan.

A Doctor Refuses to give Proper Care, and A Young Woman Dies

The next case is equally illuminating. It is a case of an Untouchable school teacher in a village in Kathiawar, and is reported in the following letter which appeared in the Young India, a journal published by Mr. Gandhi, in its issue of 12th December 1929. It expresses the difficulties he [=the writer] had experienced in persuading a Hindu doctor to attend to his wife, who had just delivered, and how the wife and child died for want of medical attention. The letter says:

> "On the 5th of this month a child was born to me. On the 7th, she [=the writer's wife] fell ill and suffered from loose stools. Her vitality seemed to ebb away and her chest became inflamed. Her breathing became difficult and there was acute pain in the ribs. I went to call a doctor—but he said he would not go to the house of a Harijan, nor was he prepared to examine the child. Then I went to [the] Nagarseth and Garasia Darbar and pleaded [with] them to help me. The Nagarseth stood surety to the doctor for my paying his fee of two rupees. Then the doctor came, but on condition that he would examine them only outside the Harijan colony. I took my wife out of the colony along with her newly born child. Then the doctor gave his thermometer to a

Muslim, he gave it to me, and I gave it to my wife and then returned it by the same process after it had been applied. It was about eight o'clock in the evening and the doctor, on looking at the thermometer in the light of a lamp, said that the patient was suffering from pneumonia. Then the doctor went away and sent the medicine. I brought some linseed from the bazar and used it on the patient. The doctor refused to see her later, although I gave the two rupees fee. The disease is dangerous and God alone will help us. The lamp of my life has died out. She passed away at about two o'clock this afternoon."

The name of the Untouchable school teacher is not given. So also the name of the doctor is not mentioned. This was at the request of the Untouchable teacher, who feared reprisals. The facts are indisputable.

No explanation is necessary. The doctor, in spite of being educated, refused to apply the thermometer and treat an ailing woman in a critical condition. As a result of his refusal to treat her, the woman died. He felt no qualms of conscience in setting aside the code of conduct which is binding on his profession. The Hindu would prefer to be inhuman rather than touch an Untouchable.

A Young Clerk is Abused and Threatened until he gives up his Job

There is one other incident more telling than this.

On the 6th of March 1938, a meeting of the Bhangis was held at Kasarwadi (behind Woollen Mills), Dadar, Bombay, under the Chairmanship of Mr. Indulal Yadnik. In this meeting, one Bhangi boy narrated his experience in the following terms :

> "I passed the Vernacular Final Examination in 1933. I have studied English up to the 4th Standard. I applied to the Schools Committee of the Bombay Municipality for employment as a teacher, but I failed, as there was no vacancy. Then I applied to the Backward Classes Officer, Ahmedabad, for the job of a Talati (village Patwari [=scribe]), and I succeeded. On 19th February 1936,1 was appointed a Talati in the office of the Mamlatdar of the Borsad Taluka in the Kheda District."

Although my family originally came from Gujarat, I had never been in Gujarat before. This was my first occasion to go there. Similarly, 1 did not know that untouchability would be observed in Government Offices. Besides in my application the fact of my being a Elarijan was mentioned and so I expected that my colleagues in the office would know before-hand who I was. That being so, I was surprised to find the attitude of the clerk of the

Mamlatdar's office when 1 presented myself to take charge of the post of the Talati.

The Karkun contemptuously asked, "Who are you?"

I replied, "Sir, 1 am a Harijan." He said, "Go away, stand at a distance. How dare you stand so near me! You are in office, if you were outside I would have given you six kicks. What audacity to come here for service!" Thereafter, he asked me to drop on the ground my certificate and the order of appointment as a Talati. He then picked them up. While I was working in the Mamlatdar's office at Borsad I experienced great difficulty in the matter of getting water for drinking. In the verandah of the office there were kept cans containing drinking water. There was a waterman in charge of these water cans.

His duty was to pour out water to clerks in office whenever they needed it. In the absence of the waterman they could themselves take water out of the cans and drink it.

That was impossible in my case. I could not touch the cans, for my touch would pollute the water, I had therefore to depend upon the mercy of the waterman. For my use there was kept a small rusty pot No one would touch it or wash it except myself. It was in this pot that the waterman would dole out water to me. But 1 could get water only if the waterman was present.

This waterman did not like the idea of supplying

me with water. Seeing that I was coming for water, he would manage to slip away, with the result that I had to go without water; and the days on which I had no water to drink were by no means few.

I had the same difficulties regarding my residence. I was a stranger in Borsad. No caste Hindu would rent a house to me. The Untouchables of Borsad were not ready to give me lodgings, for the fear of displeasing the Hindus who did not like my attempt to live as a clerk, a station above me. Far greater difficulties were with regard to food. There was no place or person from where I could get my meals. I used to buy 'Bhajhas' morning and evening, eat them in some solitary place outside the village, and come and sleep at night on the pavement of the verandahs of the Mamlatdar's office. In this way, I passed four days. All this became unbearable to me. Then I went to live at Jentral, my ancestral village. It was six miles from Borsad. Every day I had to walk eleven miles. This I did for a month and a half.

Thereafter the Mamlatdar sent me to a Talati to learn the work. This Talati was in charge of three villages, Jentral, Khapur and Saijpur. Jentral was his headquarters. I was in Jentral with this Talati for two months. He taught me nothing, and I never once entered the village office. The headman of the village was particularly hostile. Once he had said, "Your fellows, your father, your brother are sweepers who sweep the village office, and you want to sit in the office as our equal? Take care, better give up this job!"

One day the Talati called me to Saijpur to prepare the population table of the village. From Jentral I went to Saijpur. I found the Headman and the Talati in the village office doing some work. I went, stood near the door of the office, and wished them "good morning," but they took no notice of me. I stood outside for about fifteen minutes. 1 was already tired of life, and felt enraged at being thus ignored and insulted. 1 sat down on a chair that was lying there. Seeing me seated on the chair, the Headman and the Talati quietly went away without saying anything to me.

A short while after, people began to come, and soon a large crowd gathered round me. This crowd was led by the Librarian of the village library. 1 could not understand why an educated person should have led this mob. 1 subsequently learnt that the chair was his. He started abusing me in the worst terms. Addressing the Ravania (village servant) he said, "Who allowed this dirty dog of a Bhangi to sit on the chair?" The Ravania unseated me and took away the chair from me. I sat on the ground.

Thereupon the crowd entered the village office and surrounded me. It was a furious crowd raging with anger, some abusing me, some threatening to cut me to pieces with the Dharya (a sharp weapon like the sword). I implored them to excuse me and to have mercy upon me. That did not have any effect upon the crowd. I did not know how to save myself. But an idea came to me of writing to the Mamlatdar about the fate that had befallen me, and telling him how to dispose of my body in case I was killed by the crowd. Incidentally, it was my hope that if the crowd came to know that I was practically reporting against them to the Mamlatdar, they might hold their hands. I asked the Ravania to give me a piece of paper, which he did. Then with my fountain pen I wrote the following on it in big bold letters so that everybody could read it:

> "To,
>
> The Mamlatdar, Taluka Borsad.
>
> Sir,
>
> Be pleased to accept the humble salutations of Parmar Kalidas Shivram. This is to humbly inform you that the hand of death is falling upon me today. It would not have been so if I had listened to the words of my parents. Be so good as to inform my parents of my death."

The Librarian read what I wrote and at once asked me to tear it off, which I did. They showered upon me innumerable insults. "You want us to address you as our Talati? You are a Bhangi and you want to enter the office and sit on the chair?" I begged for mercy and promised not to repeat this, and also promised to give up the job. I was kept there till seven in the evening, when the crowd left. By then the Talati and the Mukhiya had still not come. Thereafter I took fifteen days' leave and returned to my parents in Bombay."

ABOUT THE AUTHOR

Dr. Bhim Rao Ambedkar, a fighter in the cause of Annihilation of Caste, was born in a low-caste Mahar family on 14th April, 1891, at Mhow cantonment, where his father served in the Army. Dr B.R. Ambedkar was born in a caste which was considered as the lowest of the low. But this very man framed the Constitution for the country. His life was one of struggles, as his radical proposals to deal with the Caste System met with overt hostility from the Upper Castes. Not only did the great Doctor fight against all institutional and social odds to keep studying, but spectacularly earned a Doctorate in Economics from Columbia University in 1917. The boy who suffered bitter caste humiliation became the first Minister for Law in free India, and shaped the country's Constitution. Dr. Ambedkar's struggle against Brahmanical Patriarchy, his radical proposals for the Hindu Code Bill, and his suggestions for a radical restructuring of property relations, alert us to his challenging of the status-quo. Dr. Ambedkar, perhaps India's most radical thinker, transformed the social and political landscape in the struggle against British Colonialism, by making the downtrodden politically aware of their own situation. Ambedkar famously said to Dalits something that bears immense importance even today - "Educate, Agitate, and Organise"...